Jeremiah Johnson

Building a Nation and Where to Build Ideal American Homes

Jeremiah Johnson

Building a Nation and Where to Build Ideal American Homes

ISBN/EAN: 9783337067601

Printed in Europe, USA, Canada, Australia, Japan

Cover: Foto ©ninafisch / pixelio.de

More available books at **www.hansebooks.com**

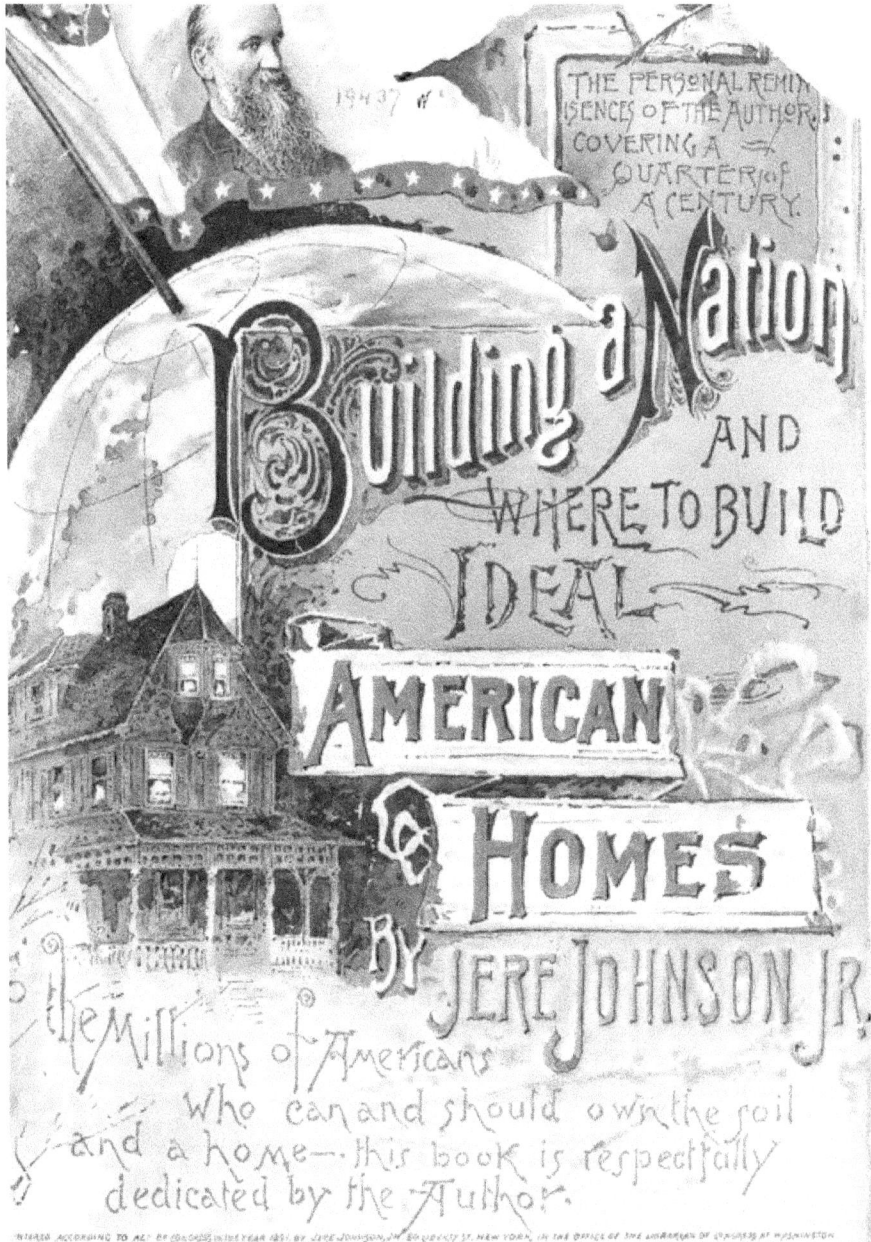

THE PERSONAL REMIN-
ISENCES OF THE AUTHOR
COVERING A
QUARTER OF
A CENTURY.

Building a Nation

AND

WHERE TO BUILD

IDEAL

AMERICAN

HOMES

BY JERE JOHNSON JR.

the Millions of Americans
who can and should own the soil
and a home—this book is respectfully
dedicated by the Author.

TITLE·GUARANTEE·&·TRUST·Cᵒ,

55 LIBERTY ST., New York.   26 COURT ST., Brooklyn.

Capital paid in,   - $2,000,000

Surplus,   -   -   -   441,293

EXAMINES AND GUARANTEES TITLES

TO REAL ESTATE.

The **RATES** for EXAMINATION, guarantee and searches, in New York, are $65 on the first $3,000, and $5 on each additional $1,000. No "EXTRAS" FOR SEARCHES. In BROOKLYN, they are $40 on the first $2,000, and $5 on each additional $1,000. No "EXTRAS" FOR SEARCHES.

The steady progress of the Company in the confidence of the public is shown by the following

COMPARATIVE STATEMENT.

	For 1888.	For 1889.	For 1890.
Income from title insurance and search business,	$152,099	$168,434	$486,925
Number of Mortgages furnished to Investors -	342	849	1,346
Amount of Mortgages furnished to Investors	$3,193,325	$6,697,288	$12,919,391

COUNSEL:

STEPHEN P. NASH.   RICHARD INGRAHAM.   GEORGE F. DEMAREST.   NEWELL MARTIN.

TRUSTEES:

GEORGE G. WILLIAMS,   EUGENE KELLY,   ALEXANDER E. ORR,   ORLANDO B. POTTER,
JOHN T. MARTIN,   JAMES D. LYNCH,   WILLIAM M. INGRAHAM,   HUGO WESENDONCK,
WILLIAM H. MALE,   JULIEN T. DAVIES,   JOHN JACOB ASTOR,   JOHN FORSYTH,
BENJAMIN D. HICKS,   EMIL OELBERMANN,   MARTIN JOOST,   JOHN D. HICKS,
ELLIS D. WILLIAMS,   SAMUEL T. FREEMAN,   CHARLES R. HENDERSON,   WILLIAM TRAUTWINE
CHARLES MATLACK.   CHARLES RICHARDSON.

JOHN W. MURRAY, PRESIDENT.   C. H. KELSEY, VICE-PRESIDENT.

LOUIS WINDMULLER, TREASURER.

FRANK BAILEY, 2D VICE-PRESIDENT.   LOUIS V. BRIGHT, SECRETARY.

TO the millions of thrifty souls who are ambitious to live in homes of their own, this book is respectfully dedicated by the author, in the hope that it will help some of them to reach the goal for which they are striving.

JERE. JOHNSON, Jr.

VIEW ON THE OCEAN PARKWAY, WITHIN HALF A BLOCK OF MY KENSINGTON PROPERTY.

Introduction.

In the following pages will be found a few personal reminiscences, covering a quarter of a century; an unvarnished description of the six attractive properties I am now offering for sale; a short explanatory article about mutual building and loan associations; and a number of practical designs for beautiful homes.

I have endeavored to render every statement clear, simple and truthful —avoiding all exaggeration.

By referring to the maps I have had prepared, the exact location of the different suburbs can be seen at a glance.

JERE. JOHNSON, Jr.,

60 Liberty St., New York.

189 & 191 Montague St., Brooklyn.

In the hope that the time will soon come when everyone will have a home of his own.

I am very respectfully,

Jere. Johnson, Jr.

A FEW PERSONAL REMINISCENCES.

I was born in the year 1827, in the old Johnson homestead, in what is now the 19th Ward of the City of Brooklyn, and near where the Naval Hospital stands. I am Dutch to the very backbone, being directly descended from Sarah Rapelje, who was the first white child born in the New Netherlands. The Dutch authorities, recognizing what an honor this was, granted the girl a large tract of land at the Wallabout. When she married in 1647, her husband presented her with a curiously wrought silver tankard, which has ever since been in the possession of the Johnson family, and which is considered one of the most valuable heirlooms in America.

My great-grandfather served bravely in the Revolutionary war as an officer in the Kings County Militia, and, for a man in moderate circumstances, is said to have loaned large sums to the patriot cause. His son, Major-General Jeremiah Johnson, is remembered as a statesman, soldier, scholar and churchman. He was thrice Mayor of Brooklyn, and was elected four times to the State Legislature. During the latter part of the war of 1812, he commanded the troops stationed at Fort Greene, Brooklyn. Barnet Johnson, my father, was a man of singularly pure and upright character, and was one of Brooklyn's foremost citizens.

And now a few words about my own career. Upon attaining my majority, I engaged in the lumber business, which I left in 1866 to become what I now am, a real estate broker and auctioneer. I at once saw what great possibilities there were in suburban property, owing to the phenomenal growth of New York and Brooklyn, and, although I have always done a large general business, I have made the selling of home sites in the outskirts of the two great cities my specialty.

The real estate men of the day were of an exceedingly conservative character. I threw aside the old, worn-out traditions. Taking for my motto, the proverb, "He who sees with his eyes believes in his heart," I held my great auctions on the very properties I had to dispose of, in order that everyone might know exactly what he was buying. Ordinary land sales are, as a rule, monotonous and tiresome. To render mine as enjoyable as possible, I introduced the then novel features of having music by such well-known military bands as those of the 7th and 23d Regiments, and of serving a really good lunch in my mammoth tent before starting the bidding.

A number of years ago, I noticed that there were thousands of wage earners who were anxious to buy home sites or to invest their savings in real estate, but who were unable to pay all at once for what they desired. To meet this demand, I secured control of some very choice property just beyond the Brooklyn city line; I issued free railroad passes in order that everyone might examine it, and I offered it in lots at low prices and on small *monthly payments*. The idea took, for in the last half decade I have sold over 20,000 lots on the monthly installment plan. This year I have even gone a step further, for at Corona and Demorest-on-the-Hilltops I am selling splendid home sites on *weekly payments*.

I have always been an optimist on the subject of advertising. Last summer it cost me in round figures, $100,000 to make known the merits of my properties through the medium of the press. Right here let me mention my flag, which has become so intimately associated with my name. There is not such another flag in the whole world. It heads most of my "ads," and is known wherever the New York and Brooklyn papers are read. It was designed for me by a very clever artist, and attracts the attention of all by reason of its simplicity and beauty. It is now protected against unscrupulous imitators by a decision of the Supreme Court.

I think that I can truthfully say I have sold a larger number of lots than any man that has ever lived; for, during the last quarter of a century, I have disposed of, either at private sale or under the hammer, at least 200,000 suburban lots, representing fully $50,000,000, exclusive of hundreds of millions of dollars worth of city real estate. Most of my operations have been confined to the States of New York and New Jersey, though now and then I have sold property in distant parts of the country. In 1886, for instance, I conducted a series of very successful auctions at Los Angeles, California.

The future of our land and city is a subject that has always appealed most forcibly to me. I remember the United States when it contained only 12,000,000 inhabitants. New York City 200,000, and Brooklyn 25,000.

Let me picture for a moment Brooklyn in 1835, when its population was scattered between Fulton Ferry and Atlantic Avenue, and when it did not extend much further than the present City Hall. Then the Common Council, as well as the different Courts, met in the Apprentices' Library Building, on the corner of Henry and Cranberry Streets. Williamsburg was a hamlet, Greenpoint contained only half a dozen farmhouses, and Hunter's Point but one. There were no railroads or omnibuses, and only a couple of hackmen. I have often crossed the East River in boats propelled by horses. The streets were lighted with oil, the dwellings with candles. Happy were the families that lived near a public pump, for there was no other water supply. Telegraphs, telephones, and indeed most of the modern labor-saving necessities, were unknown. By night, a few watchmen, called leather-heads, guarded the city, and by day the constables kept order.

In 1835, New York only extended to Second Street, and, except as regards point of size, was very little in advance of her smaller sister. The last fifty years, however, have brought about great changes. Our country has increased in population five-fold, New York ten-fold, and Brooklyn thirty-fold, and yet all three are still in their infancy. New York and Brooklyn have become rivals of the great European capitals, as far as wealth, learning and refinement are concerned, and are sure in the next few years to be consolidated into one great city.

Thousands of children are now living, who will see this the Rome of the 20th Century. Before 1950 it will contain a population of over 8,000,000 souls, and will embrace the counties of New York, Kings, Westchester, Queens and Richmond. This vast area will be densely peopled. The facilities for going from one part of the city to another will be far beyond anything our minds can now grasp. There will certainly be no surface railroads, for all tracks will be elevated or depressed. Scores of bridges will span the North and East Rivers, while beneath their waters numerous tunnels will have been constructed. All machinery will be run by electricity, of which subtle force we are just beginning to know something.

New York will be the financial center of the world, as well as the center of intellectual and social life. Its magnificent public buildings and parks, its museums and art galleries, its theatres and coliseums, will render it the Mecca of all travelers. Rich and poor will delight to live within its limits.

If anyone is inclined to ridicule me for making such a bold prophecy, I will remind him that Voltaire once called Sir Isaac Newton a "poor dotard," for daring to affirm that the time would come when men would travel at the rate of twenty miles an hour. Sixty miles in sixty minutes is an ordinary thing now-a-days. In conclusion, let me say that no one in the year of grace 1891 can begin to picture the wonderful things the future has in store for us.

JERE. JOHNSON, Jr.

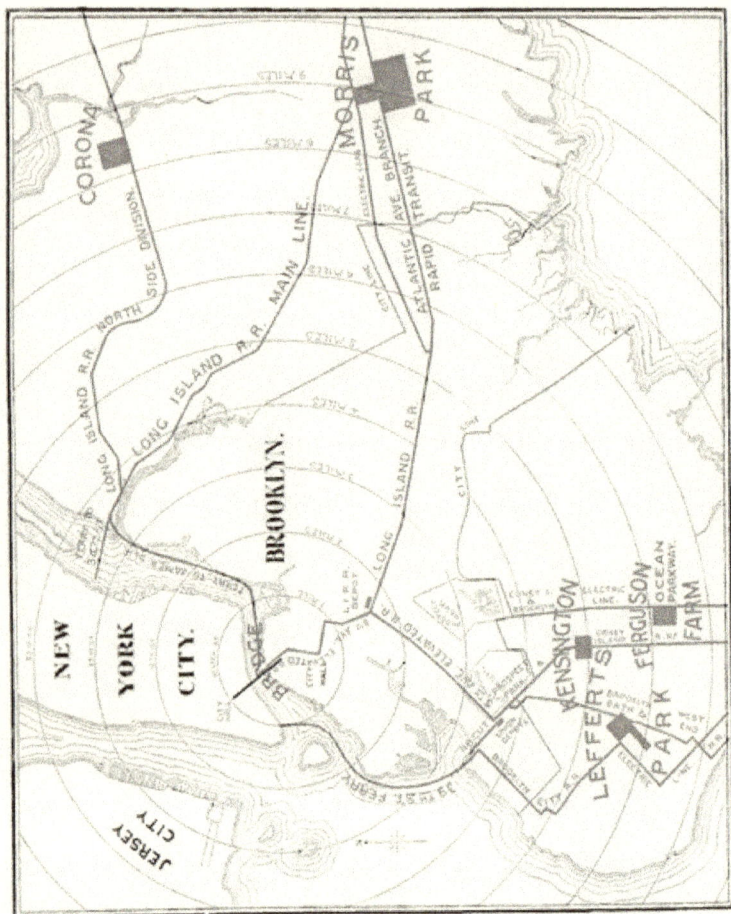

MAP SHOWING THE LOCATION OF FIVE OF MY PROPERTIES.

HOW I SELL MY PROPERTIES.

Before describing my properties minutely, I wish to present a few preliminary statements. As I have said before, I ask everyone before buying to make a careful personal examination of my lots. If this is done, there can be no deception. You see just how the land lies and all its advantages and disadvantages—provided you can find any disadvantages. Free passes to and from all properties will be cheerfully furnished on application.'

All lots may be paid for in *Monthly Installments*. If it is desired, *Weekly Payments* will be accepted at Corona and Demorest-on-the-Hilltops. Every purchase must be completed in two years from the date of signing the contract ; and installments are graded accordingly. Where all cash is paid, a discount of ten per cent. will be allowed, except at Kensington Heights and Lefferts Park, where the discount is five per cent.

The title to every lot is insured without any expense to the buyer, by the Title Guarantee & Trust Company of New York, with its immense capital and surplus of $2,500,000. This makes the purchaser absolutely secure, and does away with all necessity of lawyers. It also renders subsequent transfers both easy and inexpensive.

Rain or shine, my representatives will always be found on the different properties. Remember, I sell my lots on their merits alone.

VIEW ON FULTON AVE. AT MORRIS PARK, SHOWING THE RESIDENCES OF MR. L. B. RYAN AND MR. J. S. STOKES.

MORRIS PARK.

Lots for $150 apiece and upwards, and on Monthly Installments.

All who travel to any extent on the Long Island Railroad have contracted a peculiar habit. Several miles this side of Jamaica is the suburb of Morris Park. As the train stops here, newspapers and novels are for the moment laid aside, and everyone looks out of the window. The reason for this at once becomes apparent, for spread out before the delighted eyes of the passengers is one of the most charming and picturesque views imaginable. The universal exclamation is: "What a pretty place! what beautiful cottages what refined surroundings!"

Morris Park is situated at the junction of the Atlantic Avenue and the main divisions of the Long Island Railroad, and is about seven miles, or twenty minutes, from either Flatbush Avenue or Hunter's Point.

At Morris Park you have no long and tiresome wait when you wish to take the cars. Through trains and "rapids" run at all hours of the day and night and on very short headway. A commutation ticket for one year costs only $47, which, excluding Sundays, is at the rate of seven cents a single trip. On each division there is a neat station, in keeping with the general character of the place.

The Brooklyn and Jamaica Electric Railroad, which, as its name indi-

MY OFFICE AT MORRIS PARK.

11

cates, runs from Brooklyn to Jamaica, skirts one side of the property, and thus adds to the accessibility.

The near future has great things in store for Morris Park in the way of additional rapid transit facilities. The Long Island Railroad is soon to extend its tracks from Flatbush Avenue to South Ferry, the idea being to connect there with the proposed "Corbin Tunnel" under the East River. The Kings County and the Brooklyn-Union Elevated Railroads are, moreover, pushing forward toward Jamaica just as fast as circumstances will permit, and will eventually pass through or close to Morris Park. When all this is accomplished real estate here will be worth many times what is now asked for it.

The surroundings of Morris Park are all that any one can ask. On one side is Richmond Hill, with its handsome houses and churches, and a picturesque range of hills in the background. A few miles to the east is the famous old town of Jamaica while a broad boulevard runs in a southerly direction to Jamaica Bay.

The whole region is high and dry and is the healthiest part of Long Island. The air is delightfully cool and refreshing, and the breezes that come sweeping in from the ocean are freighted with ozone. To quote old Joanna Baillie :

> "This pure air
> Braces the feeble nerves and warms the blood,
> I feel in freedom here."

VIEW ON JEFFRIES AVENUE AT MORRIS PARK, LOOKING NORTH.

Morris Park has long since passed the embryo state. It is fully developed and adequately restricted ; and no expense has been spared in rendering it the ideal among suburbs. Any number of beautiful residences in all styles of modern architecture, and costing from $3,000 to $12,000. have been built by former purchasers. These charming homes, a few of which are shown in the illustrations, are encircled by glistening lawns embellished by bright flower beds. The streets and avenues are well kept and are bordered with superb shade trees—real shade trees, none of your little two-for-a-cent saplings that die as soon as planted.

Morris Park possesses every Nineteenth Century convenience. An elegant new public school, the finest in the whole county, has just been erected on the property, at a cost of over $15,000. Good stores and churches are of course close by. Several miles of stone sidewalks have already been laid. Water mains are found in all the streets. It is expected that electric lights will soon be introduced. An efficient fire department gives one a reassuring feeling of security. There are telegraph offices in both depots.

The residents here are refined, agreeable people, and you may rest assured that you will always have congenial neighbors. A "Citizens' Improvement Committee" has been formed among the property owners, and this is constantly on the outlook for whatever will add to the attractiveness of the place.

At Morris Park there are splendid facilities for all kinds of amusements ; games like tennis and croquet may be indulged in "*ad libitum.*" The driving in

RESIDENCE OF MR. GEORGE STARRETT, AT MORRIS PARK.

RESIDENCES OF MR. JAMES McENTRY AND MR. G. H. JORDANS, JR., AT MORRIS PARK.

the vicinity is excellent. Morris Park boasts a cozy little club house where the members while away many a long winter's evening. Such another place for children cannot be found the wide world over; and a puny girl or boy at Morris Park is as rare a sight as a white crow.

In this spot,

"Where nature spreads her fruitful sweetness round,
Breathes on the air and broods upon the ground,"

even the most fastidious are sure to be suited. If you are a man of moderate means, and yet desirous of living in a refined neighborhood, you should apply at once to me for complimentary passes and visit Morris Park. My agent will always be found in the office directly opposite the station on the Atlantic Avenue branch of the Long Island Railroad. The prices of the lots range from $150 apiece up, according to the location, and may be paid for in installments.

KENSINGTON HEIGHTS.

Lots $250 apiece and upwards, and on Monthly Installments.

Kensington has a charming name — a name, however, of which all this section is well worthy. The lots I am selling are splendidly located in the Town of Flatbush, just beyond the Brooklyn city line, on 39th, 40th, 41st, 42nd, 43rd, 44th, 45th, 46th, 47th, East Second, East Third, and West Streets; Gravesend and 16th Avenues, and Avenues D, E, and F. These streets and avenues are all well made, and every lot is ready to be built upon at once. The land is high and dry, with perfect natural drainage, and is as level as a billiard table.

Every part of the property is supplied with water in mains, and miles upon miles of substantial stone sidewalks have been laid. Several Gas and Electric Light companies are now quarreling in the Legislature for the privilege of lighting this section.

Methodist, Presbyterian, Dutch Reformed, Episcopalian, Congregational and Roman Catholic churches, as well as excellent schools, both public and private, are all close by.

15

VIEW OF PARKVILLE FROM MY KENSINGTON HEIGHTS PROPERTY.

The poet Thomson says somewhere that "Health is the vital principle of bliss." If this be so, the resident here ought to be a very happy man, for Kensington is proverbial for its healthfulness.

The surroundings of Kensington are simply delightful. Towards the north are seen the comfortable cottages of West Brooklyn, and in the distance Brooklyn itself; and towards the south the churches and houses of Parkville. 39th street is being laid out as a boulevard from Brooklyn to Kensington. Prospect Park, with its beautiful walks and drives, its sylvan glens and nooks, its glistening lakes and meadows, is about a mile distant. My property runs to within half a block of the incomparable Ocean Parkway, the finest drive in America.

Right here is the very best and most fashionable part of the Ocean Parkway, and it is right here that such famous business men as Peter H. McNulty, J. D. W. Sherman, J. J. Edwards, J. F. Graham, J. F. W. Leslie and James Armstrong have erected palatial mansions, costing from $6,000 to $25,000 apiece. Some of the gentlemen living hereabouts have just contracted for a Casino where they and their friends can bowl, play tennis and badminton, or indulge in similar innocent and health-giving pastimes to their hearts' content.

One of the first questions a prudent man asks when he examines a piece of suburban real estate is, "How about the train service?" The rapid transit facilities of Kensington would satisfy not only such a man, but also the most chronic and dyspeptic grumbler.

Kensington Heights can easily be reached from the Brooklyn Bridge inside of twenty-five minutes by taking the Fifth Avenue Elevated Railroad and changing at the Union Station, 36th Street and Fifth Avenue, for the Prospect Park and Coney Island (Culver's) Railroad. The latter line has recently built, right on my property, an expensive new depot, probably the most artistic and stylish on Long Island.

The great cut of the South Brooklyn Railroad and Terminal Company through 38th Street has been completed for some time, and it is confidently expected that trains will soon run direct from Kensington to the 39th Street Ferry for the foot of Whitehall Street, New York. This ferry, which, with its splendid equipment, is universally admitted to be the finest in the country, will then be about five minutes from the property.

Accessibility, charming surroundings, health—these are some of the inducements Kensington holds out to the home-seeker, who should remember that, if he buys a plot of ground and wishes to build, but does not possess the ready money, he can readily borrow the requisite amount from any reputable building and loan association.

STATION OF THE PROSPECT PARK AND CONEY ISLAND (CULVER'S) RAILROAD, ON MY KENSINGTON HEIGHTS PROPERTY.

RESIDENCE OF MR. PETER H. McNULTY, AT KENSINGTON.

To the investor the property must appeal just as forcibly as to the home-seeker. Flatbush will soon become the 27th Ward of Brooklyn. Taxation is very light. The whole region is being developed at a phenomenal rate. The splendid improvements on the Martense Farm and at West Brooklyn are in the immediate vicinity.

Lots may be purchased at Kensington Heights as low as $250 apiece and may be paid for in monthly installments. To fully appreciate the property, you should come to me for free passes and examine it at your earliest convenience. "The sleeping fox catches no poultry," and you may never again have such a chance to lay out your savings to so great advantage. Rain or shine, my agent will always be on hand at the Kensington depot to show the lots.

LEFFERTS PARK.

Lots from $200 apiece up, on Monthly Installments.

Lefferts Park is situated in one of the pleasantest parts of the Town of New Utrecht, and is only a short distance beyond the Brooklyn City Line. To be more definite, the lots I am selling are on 64th, 65th, 66th, 67th and 70th Streets, and 13th, 14th, 15th, Bay Ridge, Ovington and New Utrecht Avenues.

Lefferts Park is reached from the Battery, New York, in thirty minutes, via the 39th Street Ferry and the new Electric Line of the Brooklyn City Railroad Company, which has just been completed, and which runs from the 39th Street Ferry past Lefferts Park to Gravesend Bay. The fare from the property to the ferry is *only five cents.*

The best way to go from Lefferts Park to the Brooklyn Bridge is to take the Brooklyn, Bath and West End Railroad, which has a station at Lefferts Park, and transfer at the magnificent Union Depot, 36th Street and Fifth Avenue, for the Brooklyn Elevated Railroad. By this route the time to the Bridge is only twenty-five minutes.

Before long the trains of the Brooklyn, Bath and West End Railroad will also run into the immense station of the South Brooklyn Railroad and

CHURCH AT LEFFERTS PARK.

Terminal Company at the foot of 39th Street. This will give additional rapid transit facilities; and in the future will help open up the section, in which Lefferts Park occupies the most favored position, to all the advantages accruing from the proposed tunnels and other similar enterprises.

From all of the above it will readily be perceived that Lefferts Park is much more accessible for the business man or artisan, be his hours early or late, than over half of the cities of New York and Brooklyn.

"All work and no play makes Jack a dull boy." Lefferts Park is rendered doubly attractive owing to the fact that it is within a five minutes' ride by several different railroads of the famous seaside resorts of Coney Island and Bath Beach with their innumerable attractions.

Lefferts Park lies on high ground, naturally well drained, the soil being very absorbent; consequently it is free from malaria, fever, and similar diseases. The air, fresh and bracing from the ocean, is tempered and moderated by the pretty wooded ridge to the north. From several points on the property magnificent views of Gravesend Bay and also of the Atlantic may be obtained.

Simple but comprehensive restrictions assure to Lefferts Park a good class of dwellings, those already built and occupied sufficiently indicating the character the neighborhood will always bear. A number of these comfortable and tasty houses have been erected with money borrowed from mutual building and loan associations. Churches, stores and schools are found either on the property itself or immediately adjoining it.

Water of the purest kind is obtainable at Lefferts Park, and, judging from the character of the subsoil, which forms a perfect natural filter, this will be free for years to come from all contamination. The probabilities are, moreover, that within a few months running water in pipes will be supplied all over the property at prices about the same as in Brooklyn.

The sale of lots at Lefferts Park has been phenomenal, but some two hundred still remain. These are on the side nearest the new Electric Railroad, now in operation, and constitute the cream of the property. The exact route of this line was not known till last fall, so the first-comers naturally bought as close as possible to the Brooklyn, Bath and West End Railroad.

Now is the time to free yourself from the burden of paying rent, and to become your own landlord. Buy a lot, join a good building and loan association, and in a few years you will be able to have a home which will be all your own.

Lots may still be purchased at Lefferts Park for $200 apiece and upward, payable in monthly installments, or with a discount of five per cent. for all cash. Whenever you can leave your business for an afternoon, visit the property, for the trip will certainly be an enjoyable and profitable one. My office is on the corner of 66th Street and New Utrecht Avenue, and here my agent will always be found. Remember that the fare from Lefferts Park to the 39th Street Ferry, on the new Electric Line of the Brooklyn City Railroad Company, is only five cents.

HOUSE OF MR. W. W. WASHBURN, AT LEFFERTS PARK. THIS COMFORTABLE DWELLING WAS BUILT FROM ONE OF MY "DESIGNS FOR BEAUTIFUL HOMES," AND COST ABOUT $2,000.

RESIDENCE OF MR. P. H. PAGES, AT LEFFERTS PARK.

CORONA

Choice Lots as low as $75 apiece on installments of One Dollar a week and upward.

Corona is a Latin word meaning crown ; and the village is most appropriately named, for Corona is the crown of all the numerous suburbs on the North Side Division of the Long Island Railroad. Corona is four miles from Long Island City, and two miles this side of Flushing. It has the best train service of any place on Long Island, for all trains stop here, and there are trains almost every half hour. Commutation is at the rate of a little over six cents a trip. New York City can be reached from Corona in about twenty-five minutes.

In a comparatively short time, Long Island City will be connected with New York by a bridge across the East River, and also by a tunnel under it. These great enterprises are not mere castles in the air, for rich and powerful companies have been organized to carry them through. When either one is completed you will be able to go without change from Corona to the very heart of the metropolis. It is needless to say that whatever lots you buy now will then be worth many times what I am to-day selling them for.

Corona is a village of some 3,000 inhabitants. It is noted for its healthfulness, and it is said that the local doctors cannot find enough to do to keep them busy. Corona possesses every convenience. There are excellent public schools, one of which, the best for miles around, is within a few yards of my lots. The churches include the Union Evangelical Church, which has the largest Sunday School in Queens County, two Methodist Chapels, and a Catholic Church. The stores are unexceptionably good, and there are several large manufactories giving employment to hundreds of hands. Property is protected by an efficient fire department, supplemented by a system of electric alarms. The most noteworthy thing about Corona, however, is that it is a place where almost every one, from the humble mechanic to the rich Wall Street broker, owns the house in which he lives.

Splendidly located on a commanding elevation and in the very best part of Corona is the property I have just put on the market. The walk to the station is a delightful one, and is sure to be appreciated by the tired business man or woman cooped up all day in a close office or workshop.

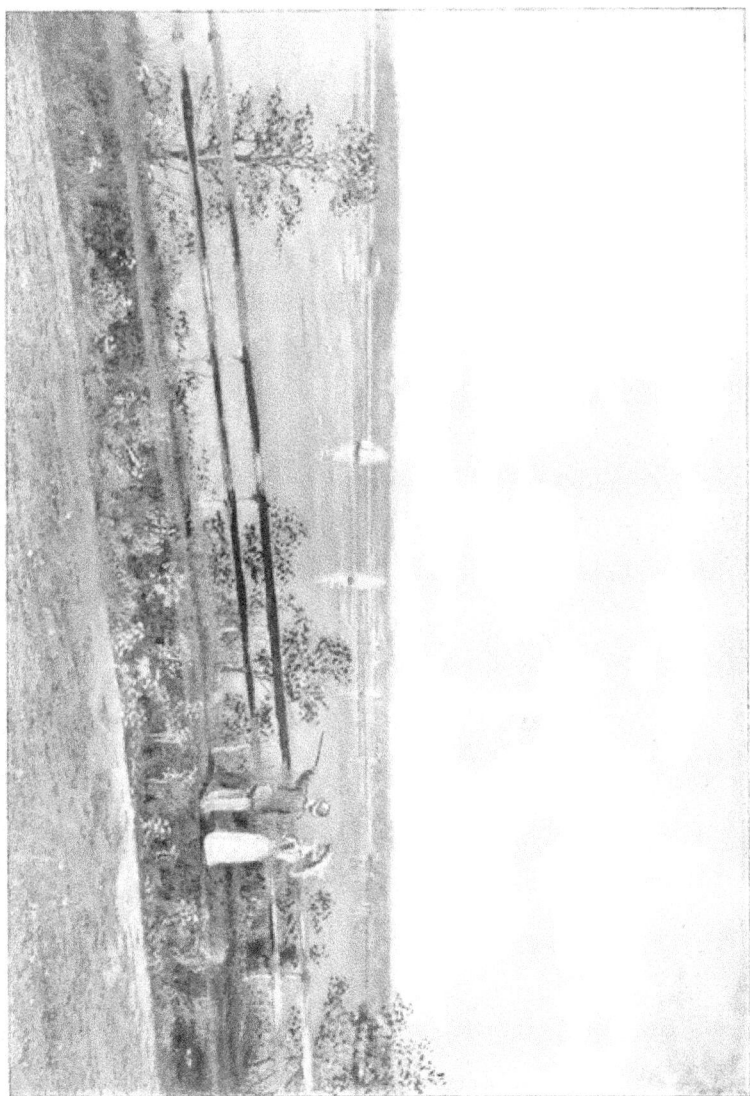

THE UNION EVANGELICAL CHURCH AT CORONA.

Many of my lots command charming views of Flushing Bay, which is a scant half mile distant, and which affords splendid facilities for every kind of aquatic sport. Jackson Avenue, macadamized all the way from Flushing to Long Island City, and by far the finest drive in the neighborhood, passes through the property. In the immediate vicinity are many handsome residences, among which may be mentioned those of C. D. Leverich, John Colton, and Frederick Schushardt. On the highest elevation of the property is the Grinnell mansion, which I am willing to dispose of at a low figure and on

24

reasonable terms. This elegant house is exceedingly commodious and is completely appointed in every particular.

Here in this desirable location, I am selling choice lots, all ready to be built upon, for *$75 apiece and upward, payable in weekly installments.* Perhaps at this point you will throw my book one side, saying : "How ridiculous! Jere. Johnson, Jr., may have good lots for three hundred or four hundred dollars apiece, but he hasn't for $75." All I reply is, don't take my word alone for the above statement, but apply to me for free passes and go to Corona and see for yourself just what my property is like.

You have probably heard the old saying, "Silks and satins, scarlets and velvets put out the kitchen fire." Bear this in mind and be economical. Give up some of your luxuries. put aside a few cents every day, and buy a lot at Corona on which to build a home. I assure you that this will be an investment you will never regret.

THE GRINNELL MANSION ON MY CORONA PROPERTY.

DEMOREST-ON-THE-HILLTOPS,

(NEAR RAHWAY.)

Very desirable lots from $25 apiece up, payable in installments of One Dollar a week and upward.

Last summer, I offered 1,253 lots at Flushing, Long Island, at prices ranging from twenty-five to one hundred dollars apiece. In four months every square inch of ground was sold, thus convincing me that the masses are after cheap property—provided, of course, it has good surroundings and is accessible. In order to supply this demand I recently secured control of a magnificent tract of land in New Jersey overlooking the flourishing city of Rahway. I have named this property Demorest-on-the-Hilltops; and, as it was purchased at a great bargain, I can here sell really choice lots for twenty-five dollars apiece and upward, and on weekly installments.

Demorest forms a magnificent plateau and is the highest ground for many miles around Rahway. The views from the property are simply superb. The city of Rahway lies right at your feet. Elizabeth, Newark, Westfield and Menlo Park (where Edison, the wizard of the Nineteenth Century, has his workshops) are in plain sight. Towards the south rise the Orange Mountains; and in the opposite direction are seen the glistening waters of the historic Kill Von Kull, and in the background the verdure-clad hills of Staten Island. At night the light from the Statue of Liberty gives one an agreeable assurance that he is not very far removed from the throbbing activity of the metropolis.

Demorest is well developed. The streets are all made, and well made too. Remsen Avenue, the thoroughfare of the property, is a splendid driveway over a mile long. Many beautiful residences are in the immediate neighborhood and there is an excellent public school within a hundred feet. Owing to its commanding elevation and to the remarkable purity of its water supply, there is no healthier spot in all Union County.

On the property are four well-built houses which will be sold on very easy terms. One of these, the Saunders homestead, is an exceedingly handsome and roomy dwelling.

The city of Rahway is about a mile from Demorest. Rahway is a manufacturing center of no mean importance. There are immense carriage and shirt factories, as well as printing press and felt works. These give employment to thousands of hands, and the man who makes his home at Demorest-on-the-Hilltops need never fear lack of work. Rahway is also noted for its handsome churches, its flourishing schools, and its well-managed stores. One of the best

26

STATION AT AVENEL, ON THE PENNSYLVANIA RAILROAD, A QUARTER OF A MILE FROM DEMOREST-ON-THE-HILLTOPS.

THE SAUNDERS HOMESTEAD AT DEMOREST-ON-THE-HILLTOPS

MAP SHOWING THE LOCATION OF
DEMOREST-ON-THE-HILLTOPS.

equipped public libraries in the state is located here. The city possesses, of course, such other conveniences as water and gas mains, sewers, electric lights, banks, and building and loan associations.

The Pennsylvania, universally admitted to be the finest railroad in America, both as regards road-bed and train service is the line you take to get to Demorest-on-the Hilltops. The pretty little depot at Avenel is within a quarter of a mile of my lots, with which it is connected by a broad avenue lined on either side with magnificent old trees. There is another station at Houtenville, half a mile from Demorest, while Rahway Junction is only about twice as far.

Demorest is the ideal location for the tens of thousands of artisans, mechanics, and salaried men, whose business calls them to Elizabeth, Newark and Jersey City, for these great manufacturing places can be reached in a comparatively short time and at trifling expense. The commutation to New York, which is within an hour's ride, is at the rate of about twenty-five cents a day, which sum, mind you, includes ferriage.

Once more I wish to say that I have A No. 1 lots at Demorest-on-the-Hilltops for $25 *apiece and upward*, payable in weekly installments. In the whole history of real estate no property, worth the taking, has ever before been offered at such figures. Remember that these are not swamp or wood lots, miles off in the wilderness, but lots high and dry, and in a beautiful and accessible suburb of New York. Free passes will be cheerfully furnished yourself and friends, on application, in order that all may inspect Demorest-on-the-Hilltops and verify every statement I have made.

A BIT OF SCENERY NEAR DEMOREST-ON-THE-HILLTOPS.

28

THE FERGUSON FARM.—OCEAN PARKWAY.

Lots from $200 up, on Monthly Installments.

This unexceptionally desirable property is located on the Ocean Parkway, about midway between Prospect Park and Coney Island, and directly opposite Howe's Hotel.

The Ocean Parkway is one of Brooklyn's greatest attractions, and every pleasant afternoon thousands upon thousands drive through the sylvan loveliness of Prospect Park and then out on its broad surface. The Ocean Parkway is five and a half miles long and two hundred and ten feet in width, and in technical language is "teferdized." The Park Commissioners have entire charge of it, and it is daily sprinkled and rolled at the public expense. On each side of the Parkway are three rows of the most magnificent shade trees on Long Island ; and, to borrow the words of a great poet, "The place seems all awave with trees."

One of the first things that impresses an observant man as he takes a spin down this incomparable boulevard is, that he has never seen a finer location in which to build a home. As far as natural beauties and advantages are concerned, the much lauded Fifth Avenue cannot hold a candle to the Ocean Parkway. Yet, strange as it may appear, lots on Fifth Avenue often bring as much as $100,000 apiece, while on the Ocean Parkway they may still be purchased for a few hundred dollars.

THE PUBLIC SCHOOL DIRECTLY OPPOSITE THE FERGUSON FARM.

The reason for this wonderful difference in price may be partially explained as follows: Up to within very recently there were no good rapid transit facilities between the property along the Parkway and Brooklyn. This drawback, how-ever, has at last been removed and the whole section rendered extremely accessi-ble. All this especially applies to the Ferguson Farm. The Coney Island and Brooklyn Electric Line passes the easterly side of the property; and, for a five-cent fare, brings one whizzing down in less than no time to Prospect Park. Here the passengers change for the Smith and Jay Street Horse Cars running to the Brooklyn Bridge and Hamilton and Fulton Ferries. An electric road is also projected along one side of the Parkway.

The Prospect Park and Coney Island (Culver's) Railroad has a station on Gravesend Avenue, about a quarter of a mile from the lots. By taking this line and transferring at the great Union Depot, 36th Street and Fifth Avenue, for the Brooklyn Elevated Railroad, the resident here can easily reach the Bridge in thirty-five minutes. When trains are run through the costly cut of the South Brooklyn Railroad and Terminal Company, as they probably soon will be, the Ferguson Farm will be within ten minutes of the 39th Street Ferry.

Sanitary experts have pronounced this section to be one of the healthiest parts of Long Island; and it is constantly fanned by refreshing ocean breezes. Coney Island is very accessible from the property, for whenever you feel inclined to take a dip in the surf, or a stroll along the beach, all you have to do is to jump into the electric cars and in a few minutes you will find yourself by "the salt sea waves."

On the Ocean Parkway, and directly opposite the Ferguson Farm, is Hiram W. Howe's. This famous hostelry is patronized by the best people in New York and Brooklyn, and here is found, as Mr. Browning puts it, "The best of welcomes, taste refined." A large public school on Coney Island Avenue is also opposite the property. Churches, stores, and other schools are found within a convenient distance ; but the resident here need not depend on any of these, for Brooklyn is so near and so easily reached that he can avail himself of the splendid religious, mercantile and educational advantages of that great city. Immediately adjoining the property is the palatial mansion and beautifully laid-out grounds of Mr. Thomas Ferguson.

Living in this neighborhood is very cheap. Taxes are low and the assessments for building the Parkway have long since been paid. The lots on the east side of East Eighth Street, and on East Seventh Street and the Ocean Parkway are all 110 feet deep. Water mains are laid on the Parkway for its entire length.

To sum up, no more favorable investment can possibly be found than on the Ferguson Farm, and it is on the Ferguson Farm that the man in search of a suitable site for a home will find just what he desires. Remember that I am still offering lots on this splendid property as low as $200 apiece, payable in monthly installments.

UNION DEPOT AT 36TH STREET AND FIFTH AVENUE, BROOKLYN, OF THE PROSPECT PARK AND CONEY ISLAND (CULVER'S) AND THE BROOKLYN, BATH AND WEST END RAILROADS. THIS ELEGANT DEPOT IS REACHED FROM THE BROOKLYN BRIDGE BY THE FIFTH AVENUE ELEVATED RAILROAD IN LESS THAN TWENTY MINUTES.

MY DESIGNS FOR BEAUTIFUL HOMES.

Every purchaser on any of my properties may select one of the designs shown in the following pages and I will furnish him with a full set of working plans and specifications *free of all charge*. A similar set would cost, if obtained from an architect, from thirty to fifty dollars.

My designs have been selected after the most careful consideration, my aim being to present only such as combine neatness, comfort and moderate cost. The prices quoted are actual estimates from reputable builders.

Many of the pretty houses on the different properties I have sold in the past have been erected from my plans; and they can be seen and examined by those interested in the subject. A large proportion of these dwellings have been built with money borrowed from Mutual Building and Loan Associations.

JERE. JOHNSON, JR.,

60 LIBERTY STREET, NEW YORK.
189 & 191 MONTAGUE STREET, BROOKLYN.

NO. 1. JERE. JOHNSON, JR.'S NEW $4,000 HOME.

NO. 2. JERE. JOHNSON, JR.'S $2,800 HOME.

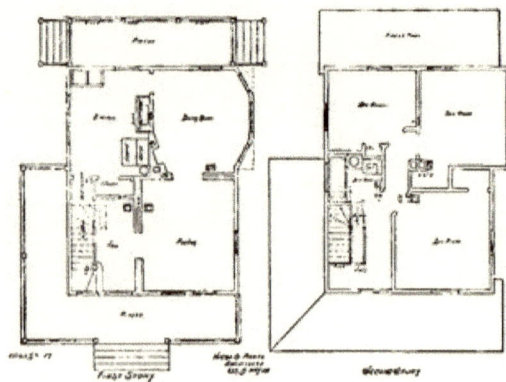

FIRST STORY

SECOND STORY

NO. 3. JERE. JOHNSON, JR.'S NEW $2,300 HOME.

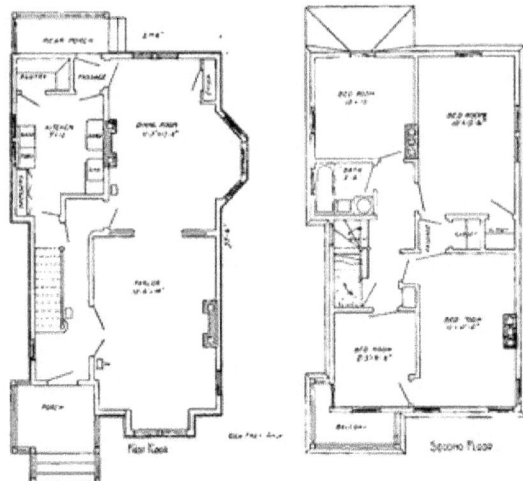

NO. 4. JERR. JOHNSON, JR.'S $3,000 HOME.

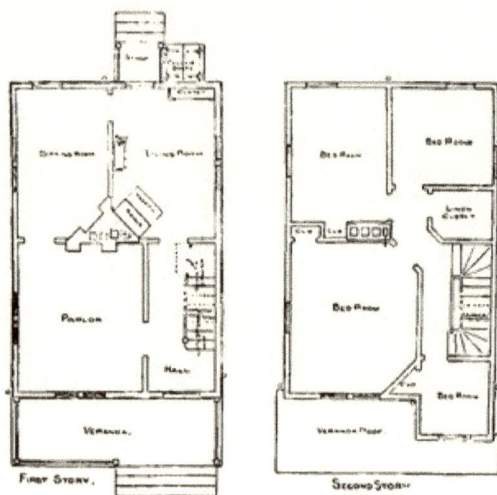

FIRST STORY.

SECOND STORY.

NO. 5. JERE. JOHNSON, JR.'S NEW $1,800 HOME.

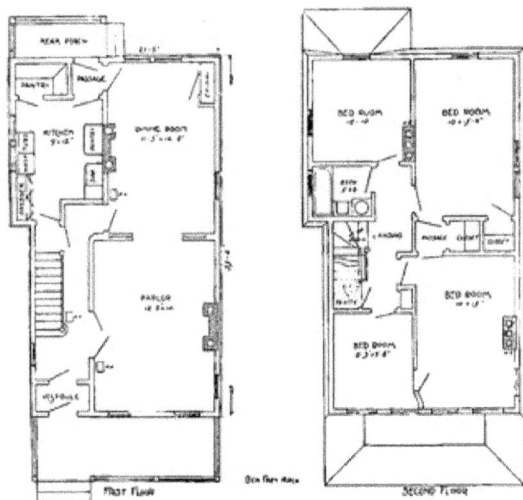

NO. 6.   JERE. JOHNSON, JR.'S NEW $1,200 HOME.

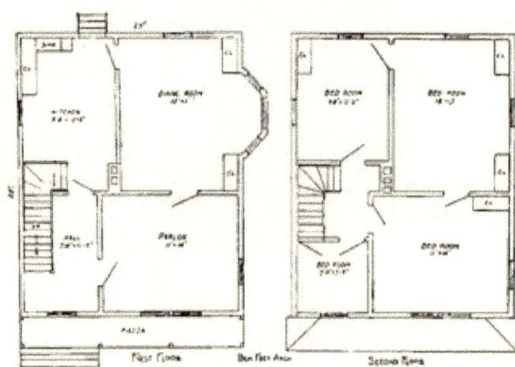

First Floor   Bay First Arch   Second Floor

NO. 7. JERE. JOHNSON, JR.'S NEW $1,000 HOME.

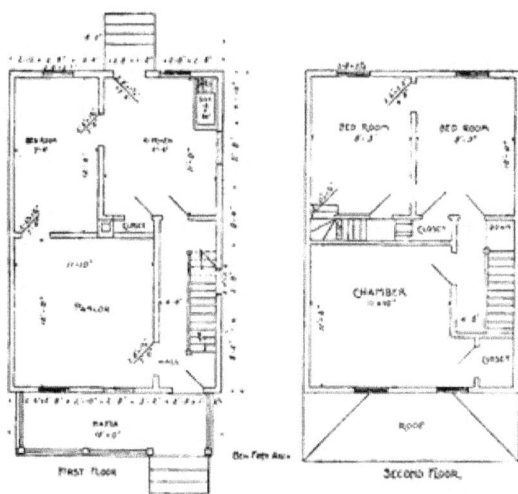

FIRST FLOOR

SECOND FLOOR

A SCOTTISH GEM AND ITS APPLICATION.

"I hae seen great anes and sat in great ha's
'Mang lords and fine ladies a' covered wi' braws :
At feasts made for princes wi' princes I've been,
When the grand shine o' splendor has dazzled my e'en,
But a sight sae delightfu' I trow I ne'er spied
As the bonny blithe blink o' my ain fireside :
    My ain fireside, my ain fireside,
    O, cheery's the blink o' my ain fireside ;
    My ain fireside, my ain fireside,
    O, there's naught to compare wi' ane's ain fireside."

What a beautiful senti-
ment, and how beautifully
it is expressed. I wish to
add that no one who pays
rent can appreciate the
full meaning of the word
HOME. My business is
the supplying of suitable
sites on which to build
homes. If you wish to
be independent of the
landlord, be sure you com-
municate with me.

My main office is at
No. 60 Liberty Street,
New York, directly oppo-
site the New York Real
Estate Exchange ; and
here is transacted the
bulk of my enormous
business. My Brooklyn
branch is room 204, on
the second floor of the
New Brooklyn Real Es-
tate Exchange, Nos. 189
& 191 Montague St., and
is in charge of James
Brumley, Jr.

JERE. JOHNSON, Jr.

THE NEW BROOKLYN REAL ESTATE EXCHANGE, 189 & 191 MONTAGUE
STREET, AND 148 & 150 PIERREPONT STREET, BROOKLYN

HOMES for ALL
JERE. JOHNSON JR.
REAL ESTATE·

CORONA.

KENSINGTON.

MORRIS PARK.

LEFFERTS PARK.

OCEAN PARKWAY.

DEMAREST-ON-THE-HILLTOPS.

JERE·JOHNSON JR·
REAL ESTATE
AUCTIONEER

APPRAISER
BROKER
STAND IN & MEMBER OF THE
REAL-ESTATE EXCHANGE (LIMITED)
AND AUCTION ROOM
NEW YORK OFFICE
60 LIBERTY ST.
BROOKLYN OFFICE
REAL ESTATE EXCHANGE BUILDING
189 & 191 MONTAGUE ST.